SAN JUAN SKYWAY

A Colorado Driving Adventure

text and photography by

SCOTT S. WARREN

SAN JUAN SKYWAY
A COLORADO DRIVING ADVENTURE

Copyright © 1990
by San Juan National Forest Association

Library of Congress Catalog Number 90-60506
ISBN 1-56044-039-2

Designed by David McKay

Additional books and materials are available through the San Juan National Forest Association. Membership supports educational and interpretive programs. For more information contact:

SAN JUAN NATIONAL FOREST ASSOCIATION
P.O. BOX 2261
DURANGO, COLORADO 81302
(303) 385-4634

In cooperation with the San Juan and Uncompahgre national forests of southwestern Colorado.

Front Cover Photo:

Driving the San Juan Skyway is a colorful experience any time of year.

Back Cover Photos:

Top: The Silverton Caldera, formerly a volcano, recalls its steamy past when filled with fog.

Middle: A snowboarder catches some air at Purgatory Resort.

Bottom: During the holiday season, Ouray Hot Springs Pool offers a popular way to relax.

Title Page Photo:

The blue columbine grows in prodigious numbers and is protected as Colorado's state flower. These were found at the base of the San Miguel Mountains.

Right:

As this stretch of the Skyway a few miles north of Telluride indicates, the San Juan Mountains take on a colorful cast during September and October.

To Jeremiah, a companion on many a San Juan outing.

I would like to thank the following people, businesses, and associations for their assistance: providing logistical support in the researching of this book have been the Telluride Chamber Resort Association, George Conley at the Coonskin Inn, David Vince with the City of Ouray, and Dan and Sandy Lingenfelter of the St. Elmo Hotel. Providing financial support has been La Plata Electric Association, Delta-Montrose Electric Association, Empire Electric Association, and the Colorado Mined Land Reclamation Division. For their expertise I would like to thank Glenn Raby, geologist for the San Juan National Forest; Brad Morrison and Dave Crawford, both with the Animas District of the San Juan National Forest; and Duane Smith, noted history sage and Fort Lewis College professor. For the use of historical photos I would like to recognize the La Plata County Historical Society, the San Juan County Historical Society, Ouray Historical Society, the Center of Southwest Studies, and again Duane Smith. For the vision in producing this book, I wish to thank Ann Bond, the San Juan National Forest, and the San Juan National Forest Association. And for her constant support, my gratitude and love goes to my wife, Beth.

The Indian blanket is one of many flowers that adds splashes of color to the roadside of the San Juans during the summer months.

The San Juans offer some of the best and most scenic trout fishing anywhere. Little Molas Lake, shown here, is situated at 11,000 feet a few miles south of Silverton.

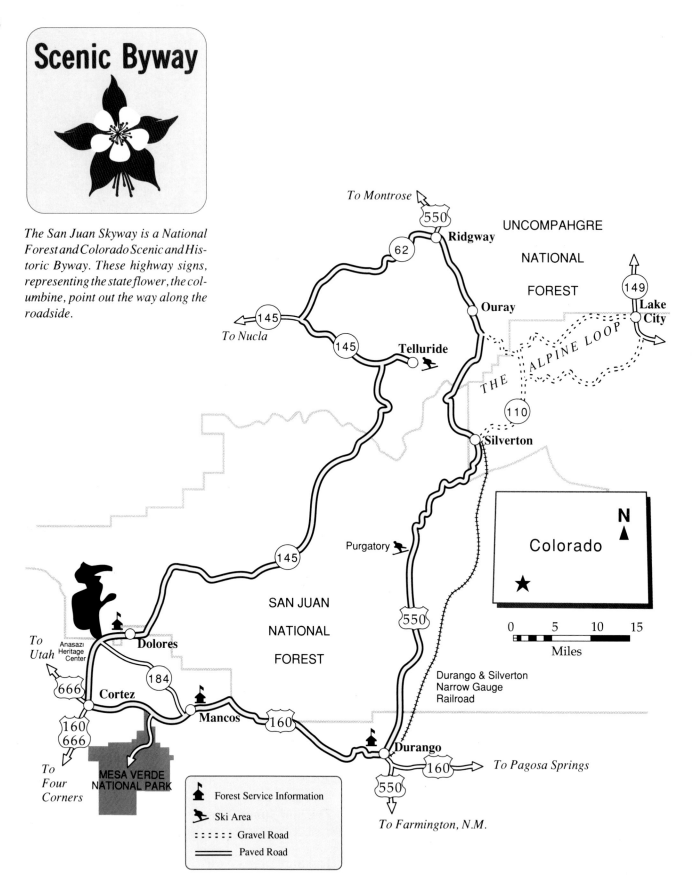

Scenic Byway

The San Juan Skyway is a National Forest and Colorado Scenic and Historic Byway. These highway signs, representing the state flower, the columbine, point out the way along the roadside.

To Montrose

550 Ridgway

UNCOMPAHGRE

62

NATIONAL

FOREST

145

To Nucla

145

Ouray

149 Lake City

Telluride

THE ALPINE LOOP

110

Silverton

Colorado

N

145

Purgatory

SAN JUAN

550

NATIONAL

0   5   10   15

Miles

FOREST

Durango & Silverton
Narrow Gauge
Railroad

Dolores

Anasazi
Heritage
Center

To
Utah

184

666

Cortez

160
666

Mancos

160

Durango

160   To Pagosa Springs

550

To
Four
Corners

MESA VERDE
NATIONAL PARK

To Farmington, N.M.

Forest Service Information

Ski Area

:::::: Gravel Road

Paved Road

p r e f a c e

In May of 1988, the United States Forest Service initiated the National Scenic Byways program as a means of promoting recreational opportunities within National Forest lands. Identifying and designating the most scenic roadways that pass through the agency's holdings, the program came in response to public needs and desires. "Scenic driving," as F. Dale Robertson, the Chief of the Forest Service, put it, "is the single most popular form of outdoor recreation on the national forests."

Over the next eighteen months, fifty-four national scenic byways were named in twenty-five states. Colorado, with nearly fourteen million acres of Forest Service lands, gained three. The first of these to be designated was the San Juan Skyway, a route that loops through the San Juan Mountains in the southwestern corner of the state. Spanning 236 miles through both the San Juan and Uncompahgre national forests, it is the longest national forest scenic byway in the nation. And, as part of a state designation program, the same route is also listed as a Colorado Scenic and Historic Byway.

Given the diversity and beauty of its namesake mountains, it makes perfect sense that the San Juan Skyway won designation as a scenic byway on both the national and state level. Not only do the San Juans stand as the largest and most rugged collection of peaks in Colorado, they also possess a treasure chest of historical relics that few others can match. From the prehistoric Anasazi to one of the West's greatest mining booms, the San Juans have witnessed a pageantry of human endeavor to match the mountains themselves.

Although mining has waned since its boom days, other resources now provide the region economic fortitude. The San Juans are an important watershed for a sizable chunk of the West. Timber harvesting and livestock grazing contribute to local economies. And most significantly, a prodigious array of recreational opportunities have made the San Juan Mountains an important travel destination for visitors from across the nation and abroad. The designation of the San Juan Skyway as a national forest scenic byway is simply the most recent proof of this.

As jagged as any in America, the San Juan Mountains stack up in an impressive juxtaposition of summits. This view looks southwest over Mineral Creek towards the Needle Range.

chapter one

WELCOME TO THE SAN JUANS

When the famous explorer John Charles Fremont gazed out across the serrated horizon of the San Juan Mountains during an expedition in December of 1848 through what is now southwestern Colorado, he was greatly impressed by what he saw. In a letter penned to his wife soon after, Fremont called them "one of the highest, most rugged and impracticable of all the Rocky Mountain Ranges, inaccessible to the trappers and hunters even in the summer time."

With part of his assessment, Fremont was not far off. Sprawling across more than 10,000 square miles—nearly a tenth of Colorado's entire land mass—the San Juan Mountains form the largest single range in the United States Rockies. With an average elevation of 10,400 feet, they are also the highest assemblage of mountains in the nation. Thirteen summits top the magical 14,000-foot mark, while many more hover just below it. And, upholding one of the greatest shares of the North American backbone, the San Juans contain an impressive 210 miles of the Continental Divide.

Such superlatives notwithstanding, the San Juan Mountains do afford one of the most impressive landscapes to be found anywhere. Spanning 360 degrees, the range marches off in a seemingly endless sea of summits. Heavily timbered canyons drop suddenly to roaring river bottoms. And breathtaking expanses of treeless tundra ramble along for miles on end. So rugged and beautiful are the San Juans, that they have for years drawn favorable comparison to the European Alps.

But inaccessible—as Fremont had claimed—the San Juans are not. Although his own ill-fated attempt at crossing them that cold December did end with the loss of ten men and 120 mules, the Ute Indians had traversed the range with ease for centuries prior. And in the decades that followed, not trappers and hunters so much, but miners inundated these mountains in search of gold. Others followed to realize livelihoods as merchants, barkeeps, and the like. Dozens of mining camps and towns sprang up in isolated valleys, on hill-

sides, and above timberline. And roads and railways were built to facilitate much needed transportation links.

Today, the San Juans still cast the same imposing stature that so impressed Fremont, but accessibility, even in a modern context, is not a prohibiting factor. Lacing the range under the azure skies of southwestern Colorado is the San Juan Skyway: a 236-mile loop drive that reveals the very heart and soul of the San Juan Mountains.

Incorporating stretches of U.S. Highways 160 and 550, and Colorado State Roads 62 and 145, the San Juan Skyway is indeed a most memorable drive. Along the way it visits the nineteenth-century mining towns of Silverton, Ouray, Telluride, and

have a safe drive

Although well maintained, the San Juan Skyway still requires a bit more respect than most roads. There are many switchbacks and dangerous precipices along the way. And weather conditions, too, can change at a moment's notice, making for hazardous driving conditions.

Here are a few rules to keep in mind when driving the Skyway. First off, stay alert. Pullouts along the way make for ideal rest stops, not to mention some great sightseeing. Obey the speed limits; they are posted for good reasons. Sharp curves can make

crossing the center line a dangerous endeavor. And last but not least, there is the weather. Summer rains can turn pavement slick. Hail occasionally piles up like snow even in spring and summer, and snow is a phenomenon that knows no seasons in the high country. From October to May, when the possibility of icy roads is greatest, conditions warrant caution and occasionally restrictions. After heavy snowfalls, the Highway Patrol may require chains or adequate snow tires on the passes, along with a good dose of common sense.

Rico, as well as the agricultural communities of Ridgway, Dolores, Cortez, Mancos, and Durango. It traverses four mountain passes, each above 10,000 feet, and skirts a like number of rivers. The Skyway tours two national forests, finds prehistoric cliff dwellings, and draws close to one of the largest tracts of wilderness in the country. The drive reveals waterfalls, stands of blazing aspen, and dizzying rock precipices. It flirts with a century-old, steam-powered train and provides passage to an exhausting array of recreational opportunities.

Because the San Juan Skyway is a fully paved, modern roadway that is open year-round, it can conceivably be driven in only a day's time. But to try to grasp the wealth of beauty along this route in so few hours would be a bit like taking in Yellowstone or the nation's capital in the same amount of time. There is simply too much to see and do.

Providing the best, and certainly the most convenient, way to witness the matchless wonder of southwestern Colorado, the San Juan Skyway is indeed one of the most dramatic drives in America. But it should serve only as an introduction to this alluring landscape. True, the story revealed along its route is a fascinating one, but it becomes even more so with every excursion made off the beaten path. Go climb a mountain, hike a trail, or stroll through a Victorian town. Take the time to enjoy a special event along the way, ride an iron horse train, or ski some powder. Soon you will discover that exploring the San Juan Skyway and the mountains that share its name can easily occupy a lifetime.

Road sign near Lizard Head Pass.

FIRE AND ICE: SAN JUAN GEOLOGY

Tugging at the skyline as they do, the San Juan Mountains have long been a catalyst for wonder to all who have gazed across them. The early Ute Indians thought them to be the handiwork of gods. Geologists, in turn, have devised their own explanations for the often cryptic lay of this tumultuous land. And while theirs may be a science clouded by a time frame measured in millions of years and by the effacing effects of erosion, their hypotheses nevertheless provide educated insight into how the San Juan landscape came to be.

In the most rudimentary sense, mountains are formed when forces deep within the earth act upon the surface above. Continental drift—a course of scientific thought that recognizes the movement of entire continents—can account for the uplifting of entire regions. The Rocky Mountain chain, and especially that portion which stretches through Colorado, marks a weak zone in the North American continental plate, and during periods of intense plate movement, stresses within the earth's crust have slowly pushed the region skyward, and continue to do so today; about an inch a year, research suggests.

Geologists theorize that the first period of mountain building in Colorado may have occurred some two billion years ago, during the Precambrian era. Although traces of these uplifts have long since vanished, it was during this time that the basement rock—the foundation of the Colorado Rockies—was formed. Constituting the oldest rocks in the San Juan Mountains, Precambrian formations today appear as quartzites in the rugged Uncompahgre Gorge near Ouray, as metamorphic gneiss in the West Needles and as the pinkish Eolus granite found in the Needles.

Following this earliest episode of construction, a long period of rest allowed erosion to grind the mountains away and make way for an influx of shallow seas. Then, about 300 million years ago,

Layers of Mancos shale and cliffhouse sandstone, both deposited on ancient seabeds millions of years ago, make up Mesa Verde. The Knife's Edge on the Mesa's north face juts boldly above the San Juan Skyway.

With the last remnants of glaciers disappearing ten thousand years ago, water is now the chief sculpting agent in the San Juan Mountains. This waterfall is at work in the Ice Lake Basin near Silverton.

during the Paleozoic era, new rumblings gave rise to an ancestral version of the Rockies. After another period of erosion, the ancient slate was again wiped clean and periodic swamps and seas followed.

During these periods of repeated floodings, deposits of silt and sand were laid down to create many of the sedimentary formations we now see along the San Juan Skyway. The red rock cliffs of the 2,000-foot thick Hermosa formation that soar above the Animas Valley are a good example, as are the colored bands along the Dolores, Uncompahgre, and San Miguel rivers. Similarly, Mancos shale, the foundation for Mesa Verde, along with the aptly named cliffhouse sandstone, were also deposited on a sea bottom.

About 65 million years ago, during a period known as the Laramide Orogeny, a renewed stirring of the continents gave birth to a number of notable mountain chains: the Alps and Andes, the Himalayas, and today's Rocky Mountains. Most of Colorado's ranges were created at this time as the result of a faulting action in the rock base. As the Precambrian substrata was fractured by stress, elongated blocks were pushed up as faulted anticlines.

Although many of Colorado's mountain ranges took shape in this manner, the San Juans resulted from a far different scenario. During the Laramide Orogeny, the area that was to become the San Juan Mountains was slowly pushed up by molten rock into a broad dome 100 miles across. Precambrian rock was exposed by erosion, leaving remnants of overlaying ocean bed deposits scattered about the dome and

along its flanks. These sedimentary layers slope away from the center of the San Juans, vividly illustrating the arc of this uplift.

Finally, about 40 million years ago, the San Juan Range erupted with grand volcanic fury. Ash, rock, and lava spewed from several huge volcanoes, forming a layer of debris nearly a mile thick in many places. Off and on for tens of millions of years the mayhem continued, leaving its distinguishing mark across the San Juan Mountains. In areas like the Needles, the overburden of volcanic debris was eventually stripped away. But across much of the rest of the San Juan highlands, a dark gray rock that once burned across the terrain is now the predominant formation. The Amphitheater above Ouray and the peaks surrounding Telluride are good examples.

Other formations resulted from the San Juan's age of fire as well. Red Mountain, for instance, was created by lava flows, but it gained its vermilion color from oxidized minerals within the rock. Igneous intrusions, or injections of molten rock into cavities within the earth, are numerous. Mount Sneffels is a dramatic example, as is Lizard Head near the pass that borrowed its name. And there are likewise grand calderas, or collapsed volcanic cones, such as the circular ring of peaks that encompass Silverton.

It was after the formation of these calderas that the San Juan Mountains were embellished with their fantastic mineral wealth. Through cracks that formed in the bedrock, mineral-laced solutions percolated up to crystallize into veins of ore. Producing more than three-quarters of a billion dollars of gold, silver, and other metals in all their years of mining, the San Juans constituted an exceptionally rich mining region. Interestingly, the best mines are found near calderas, like that of Silverton, and at the point of contact between igneous intrusions and the surrounding rock, such as the Camp Bird Mine at the foot of Mount Sneffels.

With the last breaths of fire exhausted, one final force was to act upon the San Juan Range. Erosion, in its various guises, can tear down whole mountain ranges, given enough time. Water, wind, and frost are its common agents, and they continue to chip away at the San Juans even today. But the most dramatic sculpting that took place in these mountains was that wrought by glaciers. Ice, as with volcanic fury, has played a major role in shaping the San Juan terrain.

Although the great continental sheets of ice never reached as far south as Colorado, mountain glaciers did form in the highlands of the state. Beginning

Pages 18 and 19: *The West Needle Mountains are made of metamorphic gneiss, some of the oldest rock in the San Juans. To skiers at Purgatory Resort, of course, the geologic significance of the range pales by comparison to their scenic value.*

Left: *Summer showers often produce colorful rainbows. This one frames the Lime Creek area between Coal Bank and Molas passes.*

a natural laboratory

With a billion-plus years of the Earth's history exposed, the San Juans are a great place to study geology. Universities from across the nation conduct summer field trips here for a firsthand look at how these mountains came to be. But one need not enroll in some distant school to take advantage of this natural laboratory. Fort Lewis College in Durango offers a four-year undergraduate program in geology that has earned a reputation as being one of the best in the Southwest.

Blessed with a study area like the San Juans, Fort Lewis's geology curriculum places emphasis on field work. Students get a good dose of the basics: how mountains are formed, the structure of rock formations, and the workings of erosion. They are also afforded an in-depth look at mining technology, geothermal activity, and oil and gas deposits. Graduates from the program often go on to fill top geology positions in both government and industry.

The Silverton caldera was one of many grand volcanoes that collapsed after spewing lava and debris across the range. Although all volcanic activity ceased long ago, the valley does occasionally recall its steamy past when filled with fog.

about two million years ago, during Pleistocene times, a worldwide cooling trend saw the gradual formation of central icecaps over mountain ranges like the San Juans. Covering even the highest peaks, these large icecaps were slowly pulled down canyons by gravity to scour the terrain in their wakes.

The most obvious effects of glacial activity are seen in the well-rounded cirques that head many summits and in U-shaped valleys, such as along Mineral Creek near Chattanooga. Sharply angular peaks, as well, were etched by glaciers. Most alpine lakes—Little and Big Molas Lakes are good examples—were scooped out by ice. And accumulations of gravel and rock now mark the terminus of glaciers near Ridgway and along the Dolores River above Rico. While the last of these glaciers surrendered their grip on the San Juans some 10,000 years ago, their effect has been a lasting one.

Alpine tundra, such as this stretch that drops away from Engineer Mountain, covers much of the San Juan Range. A land too high and harsh for trees to grow, tundra is instead characterized by wildflowers, low-growing mattes of forbs, and sweeping vistas.

chapter three

A WORLD OF DIVERSITY: SAN JUAN ECOLOGY

Rising some 8,000 feet above the surrounding tablelands, the San Juan Mountains pose an impressive vertical spectrum across which is found a diverse selection of plant communities. Vast expanses of sagebrush, stands of pine and aspen, spruce forests, and alpine meadows all add allure to the scenery. But, too, each constitutes an integral piece to a fascinating ecological puzzle.

The distribution of plant life in mountains like the San Juans may at first seem random, but it does follow predictable patterns that are dictated by, among other things, climate. Generally speaking, for every thousand feet gained, there is an overall drop in temperature of three degrees. A drive along the San Juan Skyway will certainly bear proof of this as temperatures on the passes are typically fifteen degrees cooler than those at lower elevations.

In response to this climatic continuum, plant types change accordingly. The pinyon pine, for example, grows in the lower country along the Skyway; it could not survive the winters of higher elevations. Similarly, Engelmann spruce trees, while thriving in frigid environs, would not last long in the dry, hot summers of the arid lands below. Grouped with other species that share similar growth requirements, these plants form distinguishable life zones.

On paper, these life zones may seem cut and dried, but the change from one to the next is never exact. Rather, it occurs over some distance. Other factors such as topography and soil add more variables. And many plants readily inhabit more than one climatic haunt. Nevertheless, life zones do offer a convenient breakdown of mountain ecology.

Reaching to about the 7,000-foot mark on the foothills of the San Juan Mountains is the Upper Sonoran life zone, characterized by little rain and lengthy hot spells. The plant types found here include sagebrush, range grasses, and the stunted forests of pinyon pine and juniper. Perhaps a barren desert to some, these dry lands constitute important ranching lands and critical winter habitat for big game. A good example of the Upper Sonoran zone is found in the vicinity of Cortez.

The Transition zone lies between 7,000 and 8,500 feet, and as its name implies, it marks the change from the low-profile plant communities of lower elevations to true forest ecosystems. Receiving more rainfall than the Upper Sonoran zone, the transition zone is able to support larger species of trees. Most common are the aromatic stands of ponderosa pine, but Gambel oak, Douglas-fir, and white fir also grow here. Between Mancos and Durango, the Skyway passes through several miles of this life zone.

Wetter and cooler yet, the Canadian zone extends up to about 10,000 feet and includes more stands of Douglas-fir, as well as those of quaking aspen. Aspen, aside from setting the hills ablaze each fall, are the only deciduous trees to fully inhabit the Rocky Mountains. They usually grow from massive root systems, which explains why whole patches will change color simultaneously. They are also the first trees to invade areas disturbed by logging and forest fires, a factor that accounts for their abundance along some stretches of the Skyway, such as in the Lime Creek area.

The Hudsonian zone encompasses the thick forests of Engelmann spruce and subalpine fir that precede timberline which, in the San Juans, is around 11,500 feet. The Hudsonian zone typically receives twice as much snow as the Canadian zone, but its growing season is short. Open meadows, or parks, are occasionally interspersed among these forests and they host a plethora of wildflowers, such as Indian paintbrush and blue columbine. Colorado's state flower, blue columbine, was once picked to the point of disappearing in many areas. Now protected by law, it is again a common jewel among all Colorado mountains. Favorite haunts of the blue columbine include Lizard Head and Molas passes.

Beyond 11,500 feet is a land which trees can no longer tolerate, known as the Alpine life zone. Because of long-term cold, snow, and blasting winds, only the hardiest grasses and forbs can successfully colonize this harsh land. Some of these species are also found in the arctic regions of the globe and among Old World mountains. Growing close to the ground, they are able to make use of an incredibly short growing season by blooming at seemingly a moment's notice. Hence, spectacular floral displays occur in these regions in late July and August. More so than with other life zones, alpine tundra is quite fragile and should be treated with care. Topping out at 11,000 feet on Red Mountain Pass, the Skyway falls just short of this last life zone, but a short walk higher would easily remedy the situation.

The Alpine Sunflower is one of the many wildflowers that thrive in summertime meadows in the San Juan Mountains. This one was photographed in Ice Lake Basin.

i m p r o v i n g   o n   n a t u r e

On occasion you may see a column of smoke rising from a distant ridge-top or mountainside. If it happens to be spring or fall, chances are the source of that smoke may actually be a deliberately caused fire, or a "prescribed burn."

Fire, in a natural state, can be a menace to forest ecosystems, but a planned or prescribed fire is a handy management tool often used by the Forest Service. When stands of Gambel oak and other undergrowth become too thick, they stop producing forage for deer and elk. But when this growth is removed through prescribed burning, succulent new growth provides a more nutritious and abundant food source for wildlife. The Forest Service, when undertaking prescribed burning, often does so in the spring or fall, when the moisture content is high and the wildfire threat is low. Precautions are taken to contain the burn area beforehand with fire breaks. These fires are kept in check, so as not to damage larger trees. And such burn areas are usually located on south-facing slopes where the sun can melt the snow in the wintertime so that animals can find the food. The amount of winter forage is a limiting factor for deer and elk populations, and by fostering more of it, the Forest Service is helping to maintain the health of the herds and create a better distribution of feeding areas.

One ecosystem that transcends elevation changes, but is an integral part of the ecology of the San Juan Mountains, is the Riparian zone. Found along stream and river banks and around ponds and lakes, the riparian world is dependent on a steady supply of water. Among lower elevations of the Skyway, large cottonwood trees are often found, as well as a variety of shrubs. At higher elevations, willows are common. Most Riparian zones result in a thick growth, constituting important habitat for a variety of wildlife.

Because so many diverse ecosystems are found in the San Juans, these mountains also provide suitable habitats for a multitude of wildlife species. Some creatures, such as mule deer, range freely across all life zones while others follow seasonal patterns, staying high during the summer and escaping to lower levels with the first snows. The majestic elk is one such creature. Widely acclaimed for their numbers, San Juan elk are often seen congregated in ranchers' fields during the wintertime.

Some species, on the other hand, stay put in one or two life zones throughout their lives. Bighorn sheep inhabit parts of the San Juan uplands, though their numbers have declined in recent years. And mountain goats, while not indigenous to the San Juans, now reside among the highest peaks of the Needles thanks to a transplant project in 1971. Currently numbering in the twenties, these goats accept handouts from backpackers during the summer, but in the winter feed exclusively along ridge tops exposed by wind.

Although their ranks have been decimated in the last hundred years, predators still fulfill an important role in the ecological balance of the San Juans. Most prevalent is the coyote, whose crafty ways confound sheep herders but help keep rodent populations in check. Bobcats live in the San Juans, but are rarely seen. Cougars constitute an even rarer sighting here. And black bears roam many forested canyons. Winged hunters include owls, hawks, and during the winter months along river courses such as the Animas, bald eagles.

While spotting large game is exhilarating, lesser creatures should not be overlooked. Chipmunks and Clark's nutcrackers, or "camp robbers," are a big hit in campgrounds. A fascinating rodent found among ponderosa forests is the Abert squirrel with its tasseled ears. And among higher elevations, marmots and pikas are readily spotted, sunning on rocks and broadcasting high-pitched chirps.

Since being transplanted into the Needles in 1971 by the Colorado Division of Wildlife, mountain goats have steadily increased their numbers and become a common sight for visitors to Chicago Basin.

chapter   four

THE SAN JUANS THEN

If a single date were to be identified as the most significant in the history of the San Juan Mountains, it would be that of September 13, 1873. On that fateful day, after lengthy negotiations, Chief Ouray and a council of Ute Indian tribal leaders signed the Brunot Treaty. Handing over a four-million-acre tract of the San Juan Mountains to the U.S. government, the agreement opened the way for a literal flood of newcomers in search of gold.

For their part, the Utes were simply bowing out of a potentially explosive situation the best way they knew how— peacefully. Driven as much by greed for mineral wealth as by manifest destiny, white prospectors had been infiltrating the San Juans with ever-increasing frequency following the discovery of gold near what is now Silverton in 1860. And the Utes, realizing they had little recourse, approved yet another in a trail of treaties that gobbled up their once-great domain, millions of acres at a time.

Called the "Blue Sky People" by other Native American tribes, the Utes—a loose assemblage of seven separate bands— had originally roamed all of Colorado's western two-thirds and parts of adjacent Utah and New Mexico. Some anthropologists conjecture that they, like the Navajos, arrived relatively late in the Southwest, around 1500 A.D., after moving down from northern Canada. Other academics are now theorizing, though, that the Utes may have been in the area much longer. What is known is that prior to their arrival, southwestern Colorado was inhabited by the Anasazi, a Navajo word that means "Ancient Ones" or "Enemy Ancestors." The Anasazi are believed to be the forebears of today's Pueblo cultures in New Mexico and Arizona.

Residing among the arid canyons and mesas of the region, the prehistoric Anasazi are best known for their elaborate cliff dwellings, the largest of which is found in Mesa Verde National Park. Cliff Palace is

Among the canyons of Mesa Verde National Park, the prehistoric Anasazi Indians built their greatest cliff dwellings. Rising a few miles from the towns of Cortez and Mancos, Mesa Verde has helped to make the area an archaeological mecca of the Southwest.

believed to have housed some 250 people at its height around 1,200 A.D. Developing a complex farming society, the Anasazi were adept at irrigation, pottery, and astronomical observation. But, for reasons that will never be fully understood, they abandoned their homeland during the thirteenth-century for areas to the south. A drought did occur at this time, and hostile tribes were putting pressure on these peaceful farmers. Similarly, a burgeoning population may have wrought ecological disaster on the land that had supported them. For whatever reasons, their picturesque homes were left to the ravens and pack rats and to archaeologists who would follow some 500 years later.

The Utes, unlike the sedentary Anasazi, were hunters and gatherers who fully inhabited the higher reaches of the San Juans. Upon their first contacts with Spaniards and horses in the early 1600s, they took to these "magic dogs," as the Utes called the beasts of burden, quite readily. And when the Spanish missionary expedition of Dominguez and Escalante passed through in 1776, the Utes greeted the party civilly. Considered to be the first fully documented exploration of the San Juan country, its intent was to find passage to the missions in California. Aside from writing down descriptions of the countryside and the Utes themselves, Father Escalante named Mesa Verde, the Dolores River, Animas River, and many other landmarks.

During the first half of the 19th century, others frequented the San Juans, mostly at random. Mountain men trapped the rivers and, while no vivid accounts of their adventures emanated from this part of the West, these wayward explorers did pave the way for others. In 1848, a trapper by the name of Bill Williams led John Fremont in his faltering attempt to traverse the range.

By 1860, a new breed of adventurer was infiltrating the San Juans. Along the upper Animas River, a man by the name of Charles Baker found the few flakes of gold that conceived the longest lasting mining booms the West had ever witnessed. And, while thirteen years would pass before the Utes relinquished control

of the San Juan Mountains, within a year of signing the Brunot Treaty, an estimated 4,000 treasure seekers had spilled into these rugged peaks. In the midst of it all, several towns sprang up almost overnight. Silverton, one of the first, quickly grew to be a town of boisterous repute.

From a prospector's assertion that the mountainsides didn't contain much gold but rather "silver by the ton," Silverton earned its name. Certainly, it was silver that propelled the town through the riotous years. Claim jumpings, shootings, and vigilante groups were common. For a time, the community boasted some three dozen saloons, all open twenty-four hours a day. Most of these, along with other houses of iniquity, lined infamous Blair Street. As if to counter these shady elements, several churches went up on Reese Street, two blocks west.

For a time, Silverton vied for prominence with other towns along the upper Animas. Howardsville, a few miles upstream, was the first seat for San Juan County. Eureka boomed to 2,000 residents at its height. And Animas Forks, situated at 11,300 feet, claimed the highest post office in the nation. All eventually became ghost towns, however, as they lost residents to a centrally located Silverton.

Just as Silverton anchored one mining district, other towns followed similar patterns of development in other parts of the San Juans. Ouray, named after the Ute leader, appeared on the northern tier of the range. Benefiting from the opulent Camp Bird Mine, Ouray was graced with a variety of fanciful architectural embellishments. Telluride was conveniently centered among several rich mines at the headwaters of the San Miguel River. And Rico sprang up along the upper Dolores River.

While life in these early mining towns may have been rip-roaring, it was not without hardships. Severely isolated from the outside world, especially during the winter months, the towns had a real need for dependable transportation. One who filled that need was Otto Mears, a Russian immigrant of small stature but indomitable ambition.

Top: *The Circle Route Stage operated on Mears' famous toll road through the Uncompahgre Gorge between 1883 and the 1920s. (Courtesy of the Ouray County Historical Museum and the Marvin Gregory collection.)*

Bottom: *This view of the interior at the Gold King mill near Silverton taken in 1905 shows boilers and the men who operated them. (Courtesy of the San Juan County Historical Society.)*

Top: *Dr. Jesse Fewkes, an early archeologist who worked at Mesa Verde National Park, stands before a collection of artifacts and the Mesa Verde Museum. Opened in 1917, this museum was a first for the National Park Service. (Courtesy of Mesa Verde National Park.)*

Bottom: *Like most 19th century towns in the San Juan Mountains, Durango took on a remarkable air of urbanity in its early days. This trolley ran between Durango and Animas City at the turn of the century. (Courtesy of the La Plata County Historical Society.)*

operation respect

No one can deny the beauty of the San Juans' countless mining antiquities. Left to the winds, these old mine shafts, cabins, and structures have faded to become picturesque memories. But their charm aside, they also pose a danger to the overly curious.

Entering old mines and mining buildings, as statistics have proven, is risky business. Rotting timbers can give way at any moment, hidden vertical shafts can lead to a fall of hundreds of feet, and deadly fumes may be present, especially in coal mines. Established to inform the public about such dangers is Operation RESPECT, a cooperative venture by the Colorado State Office of the Bureau of Land Management and Women in Mining. Through education and the closure of mines, their efforts have helped make people aware of the dangers that old mines pose. But too, as the name suggests, the program is concerned with promoting respect for these antiquities as private property.

Many visitors to the San Juan Mountains do not know that most mines are privately owned. Around Silverton and Telluride, and along Red Mountain Pass, a scan of a Forest Service map will reveal a patchwork of private lands. These are patented mining claims established years ago, and entering them does constitute trespass. Removing old pieces of equipment or construction materials is an act of theft. Mining relics found on public lands are protected as cultural resources, and taking them is likewise a felony. For safety's sake and out of respect for private property, the abandoned mines and mine structures that dot the San Juan Mountains are best enjoyed from a distance.

This old mine is found in Chicago Basin.

Upon building his first toll road, Mears quickly realized the inherent opportunities of providing such a basic necessity to miners. With the bulk of his routes traversing southwestern Colorado, he became known as the "Pathfinder of the San Juan." His most dazzling success was the Ouray-to-Red Mountain route that climbed the rugged Uncompahgre Gorge just south of Ouray. Completed in 1883, this road was eventually widened and became known as the Million Dollar Highway, a reference—some say—to the cost of construction, while others insist it reflects the value of ore-bearing fill that was used in the roadbed. Today, the San Juan Skyway follows this same route.

The need for reliable transportation also attracted railroads to the San Juans. Under the direction of General William Jackson Palmer, the Denver and Rio Grande Railroad constructed a network of narrow gauge lines throughout these mountains. The Durango to Silverton segment greatly changed life for Silvertonites upon its completion in 1882. Offering a real sense of permanence, the train ushered in a boom that led to one of the state's largest breweries and the Grand Imperial Hotel. Still in service today, the Durango and Silverton Narrow Gauge Railroad carries

tourists, instead of mineral ore, along the same forty-five miles of track.

On the fringes of the range, at elevations with adequate growing seasons, other municipalities were established to supply the mining districts beyond. Often matching the mining towns in prosperity, these communities realized handsome profits by producing food for the miners. Ridgway, Dolores, Cortez, and Mancos all have roots as ranching or farming towns, as does Durango. But Durango grew to be much more.

First established as Animas City in the 1870s, Durango proper took shape in 1881, with the arrival of the Denver & Rio Grande Railroad. Foolishly, Animas City played hardball with General Palmer who, in turn, built his depot two miles south, establishing the new town of Durango. In a short time, Durango swallowed Animas City whole. Aside from enjoying prominence as a transportation hub, Durango also prospered from nearby coal deposits.

For many years, economic prosperity in the San Juan mining districts showed no signs of relenting, but in 1893, the literal bottom fell out as silver prices dropped from $1.29 per ounce to $.40 almost overnight. Many towns soon became only faded memories, but the best did survive. Silverton, for instance, again realized the benefits of its rich ore deposits, as evidenced by the construction of its grand County Courthouse in 1907 and the Town Hall a year later.

A devastating flu epidemic swept through the San Juan area in 1912, killing many. Many mines quit producing. Further devaluations of silver had devastating effects on the area's mining industry, as did World War II. Eventually, the "Song of the Hammer and Drill," as historian Duane Smith so eloquently put it, fell mostly silent.

Above: The Durango & Silverton Narrow Gauge Railroad has made the run from Durango to Silverton along a forty-five mile stretch of the Animas River since 1882. It is shown here, ready to leave the Durango station.

Adding a new way to visit the wilderness are llamas, a member of the camel family that hails from South America. With several llama breeders and outfitters located in the San Juans, these gentle beasts are becoming a more common sight in southwestern Colorado. These two met at the first annual Llamathon held near Mancos.

chapter five

THE SAN JUANS NOW

Although only a handful of mines are still in operation, the San Juan Mountains nevertheless provide economic vitality to area residents. But unlike their finite mineral wealth, most of the resources reaped in the region today are renewable. That is, they can be replenished to provide additional benefits for generations to come. The key to successful utilization of these renewable resources, however, is proper management. Today, that is the goal of the federal government agencies which hold title over most of the San Juan Mountains.

Established in 1905 by proclamation of the president, the San Juan National Forest encompasses 1.9 million acres of southwestern Colorado, including most of the land visible along the Skyway. The Uncompahgre National Forest, also established in 1905 and encompassing more than a million acres, covers the northern reaches of the route. Under the auspices of the United States Department of Agriculture, the San Juan and Uncompahgre national forests—along with the Bureau of Land Management (BLM), a Department of Interior agency—practice what is known as "multiple use" management of these lands. Realizing that the resources under their care can serve many needs, the Forest Service and BLM strive to insure that everyone benefits.

Of course, one of the pillar principles behind this management scheme is that most of these resources are renewable. Timber is one such commodity. After careful harvesting, mature trees can be replaced by planting new ones. While San Juan forests are not the virtual tree-growing lands that those in the Pacific Northwest are, some areas along the Skyway do work well as timber-producing lands. North of Dolores is ideal for growing ponderosa pine, while Missionary Ridge near Durango has supplied several thousand board feet of spruce and fir. Aspen trees are likewise harvested in great numbers near Mancos.

Another renewable resource is forage. For ranchers, rangelands interspersed among most reaches of the San Juans provide feed for cattle and sheep during the summer months. Under national forest management, livestock is constantly moved to minimize impact on any one area. While some hikers balk at finding cows or sheep in the back country, grazing, when properly managed, can be a wise use of the land's bounty.

Other natural resources are managed in the San Juan Mountains as well. With seven major rivers finding their sources here, the San Juans are an important provider of water for much of the Southwest and for places beyond, such as Los Angeles. And, while hunting and fishing are regulated by the Colorado Division of Wildlife, the Forest Service does work to improve wildlife habitat in many ways.

Given the delicate balance that nature so often strikes in the San Juans, multiple use management practices must always weigh the consequences of any action taken. When these actions are ignored, the costs can be high, as mistakes in years past have taught us. Timber clear-cuts just below timberline have proved nearly impossible to replant. And erosion caused by severe overgrazing decades ago led to the silting of fish habitat downstream. Today, having learned from such faux pas, land managers are considerably more successful in determining the wisest use of resources.

In recent years, yet another utilization of the land has risen sharply. Actually considered a renewable resource, recreation has taken on many forms and fashions in the San Juans, and today it represents the most important economic benefit these mountains provide.

Given the splendor of the San Juan Mountains, it is not surprising that people would flock to this corner of Colorado from across the nation and abroad. But how these visitors enjoy this beauty is another thing. Many come simply to hike the back country of the San Juan's many wilderness areas—lands officially set aside as a haven from vehicles and other intrusions of civilization. The largest, the 500,000-acre Weminuche Wilderness Area, spans a vast chunk of the range.

Hunting and fishing are two pastimes with time-honored traditions here, as are mountain climbing, four wheeling, and skiing. Two downhill ski resorts, Purgatory and Telluride, have provided destination skiing terrain for more than a quarter century. Whitewater rivers have thrilled kayakers and rafters alike for many years. And mountain running has comparatively venerable roots in the San Juans. Silverton's Kendall Mountain Run is said to have started as a contest between two miners around the turn of the century to see who could reach the summit first. Although not a sanctioned race until 1978, the event, along with the Imogene Pass Run, challenges the very limits of athletes on an annual basis.

Forage for sheep is a good example of a renewable resource. On national forest lands, the animals are constantly moved so that overgrazing does not occur. The plant life can then grow back with no damage to the ecosystem.

Inset: Junior Chavez, a sheepherder of Navajo descent, has herded sheep in the San Juan Mountains for many years. While his is often a lonely existence, it is one that is filled with many rewards as well.

In recent years, new recreational pursuits have gained attention in the San Juan Mountains. Telluride and Silverton host hang gliding events each year. Cortez and Durango witness annual gatherings of hot air balloons. And bicycling has taken on a new aspect in the 1980s. As evidenced by the establishment of the Durango Wheel Club in the early 1890s and the Iron Horse Bicycle Classic in 1972, road cycling has been around for a long time. But in 1983, a hybrid pedaling machine, the mountain bike or all-terrain bicycle (ATB), has taken to the non-wilderness trails and back roads of the San Juans. Durango, with its annual hosting of important mountain bike races and its resident crew of professional competitors, has become the Rocky Mountain capital for the sport.

As the realization of southwest Colorado's recreational potential continues to unfold, the Forest Service and BLM have turned more of their attention towards satisfying the needs of an ever-growing number of forest users interested in enjoying the great outdoors. These agencies see this not only as an opportunity to instill respect for the land in the public, but also as a way of working hand in hand with local governments and businesses to promote the economic mainstay of the region—tourism.

Many who visit southwestern Colorado come simply to answer the siren call of one or more of the region's major attractions: the Durango & Silverton Narrow Gauge Railroad, Mesa Verde National Park, the region's two fabled ski resorts, or Black Canyon of the Gunnison National Monument to the north. But in so doing, they soon learn about many of the other allurements worth experiencing. Some extend their visits to take it all in, and many vow to return in the future.

Given southwestern Colorado's prodigious array of sights and attractions, its wealth of recreational opportunities, and its scenic wonders, it indeed makes sense that the San Juan Mountains are today a favored vacation spot for folks from all over. And now, with the San Juan Skyway established, people have yet another reason to visit.

A recreation specialist for the San Juan National Forest prepares to blast a rock on the Purgatory Creek Trail. Recreation is just one use that the Forest Service addresses in multiple use management of the land.

giving   disability   a   possibility

While the array of recreational opportunities available in the San Juan Mountains is comprehensive, so too is the clientele that can take advantage of it, thanks to the Durango/Purgatory Handicapped Sports Association (D/PHSA).

Established in 1983 by Dave Spencer, D/PHSA was one of the first programs of its kind in the nation. Since then it has taught over a thousand physically and mentally challenged persons of all ages how to ski on the slopes of Purgatory. Spencer—who himself lost a leg to cancer—realized that mastering a sport can go a long way towards building self-esteem. And because ski equipment can be easily adapted to meet special needs, skiing was the ideal sport for disabled individuals to learn. As Sue Ehrhardt, one of the program's first students, put it, "Skiing gave me the wind in my face."

Although Dave Spencer passed away in 1986, his dream is strong and still growing. Staffed by over eighty trained volunteers and funded by generous donations and fundraising events, D/PHSA has been able to expand its winter program over the years. And, with the help of the San Juan National Forest and Outward Bound, students now enjoy hiking, camping, climbing, rafting, and much more after the snow has melted. By

striving to "give disability a possibility," the Durango/Purgatory Handicapped Sports Association has become an integral part of the San Juan community.

A volunteer and disabled athlete enjoy skiing at Purgatory Ski Resort.

*Recreation now constitutes the most popular
use of the San Juans. This kayaker is
competing in Durango's Animas River Days,
a whitewater competition held each June.*

While roadside beauty is plentiful along the San Juan Skyway, the wise traveler will take the time to explore side roads and trails. This hiker has the fall splendor of the Ophir Pass road all to herself.

chapter six

BUCKLE UP AND TAKE A RIDE

The story of the San Juans is one of a vast and beautiful landscape and the people who have lived, worked and played here. The Skyway, for its part, celebrates this timeless union. Along this 236-mile ribbon of pavement, tales are told in bold and believable fashion. Fantastic dramas of geology and ecology unfold. Echoes of the past mesh with the pageantry of the present. And always reeling along in a continuous panorama, a sublime land inspires wonder in all who pass.

Here, then, is a guide to the San Juan Skyway. Although you can begin at any of several points, this tour starts in Durango, the largest community along the route. It follows U.S. Highway 550 north to Ridgway, where it turns west on State Highway 62. At Placerville it turns south on State Highway 145 to finally pick up U.S. Highway 160 in Cortez for the return leg to Durango. Along the way, there is much to see and do—far more than this text could possibly cover. Prudent advice, then, suggests that you look beyond the sights and attractions mentioned here and make some discoveries for yourself. Stop in at the visitor centers or Forest Service district offices in each town. Strike up conversations with the locals. Venture down side roads and trails. Explore beyond the beaten path. That is, after all, one of the inherent pleasures of driving a route like the San Juan Skyway.

Situated along the banks of the Animas River, on the southern flank of the San Juan Mountains, Durango is a pleasurable mix of tradition and trend. For over a century, the town has come to relish the almost mournful din of the whistle that announces the comings and goings of the Durango & Silverton Narrow Gauge Railroad, the D&SNGR. Durango also embraces exquisite examples of Victorian architecture found along Main Avenue, on East Third Avenue, and scattered about other parts of the city. But just as

Durango is mindful of its past, so too is it willing to accept the nuances of contemporary times. A splash of color in a store window hints at the town's growing allure to shoppers. And a flash of color on the street signifies its growing prominence as a sports Mecca. Clad in multi-hued outfits, mountain bike enthusiasts have discovered Durango's abundance of great riding terrain. Some resident racers have even gone on to earn notable acclaim.

Beyond Durango, the Animas Valley opens up into a broad expanse of pastures and river bottom. The Animas River, its full name the "Rio de Las Animas Perdidas" or "River of Lost Souls," meanders wildly about the valley floor, leaving oxbow ponds in its wake. Legend has it that a member of the Dominguez-Escalante expedition drowned in the river, but its distracted course likewise explains the colorful name.

For ten miles the Skyway cuts a straightaway course through the valley (paralleling the narrow gauge tracks for much of the way) before starting the long climb into the mountains. Prior to this grade change, the Hermosa Creek drainage opens up. With 85,000 acres of timbered canyons, the "Hermosa," as locals call it, is managed by the San Juan National Forest as a roadless area. While this tract of back country shares many of the same characteristics that designated wilderness areas boast, it is considerably less crowded.

Seven miles and about a thousand vertical feet further up the road is the turn-off for Rockwood. This is the last railhead along the D&SNGR before its tracks disappear into the rugged Animas River Gorge. From here, backpackers can catch the Animas River Railbus, a diesel-powered "commuter" line designed especially for visitors to the Weminuche, Colorado's largest wilderness area. From Needleton, the most popular departure point for the Railbus, hikers file into the spectacular environs of Chicago Basin during the summer season.

Beyond Rockwood, the Skyway climbs past Tamarron, a renowned golf resort, revealing alluring glimpses of the Needle Mountains—the heart of the Weminuche Wilderness Area. The two most prominent peaks visible are Pigeon and Turret, each above 13,000 feet. Just beyond, however, rise Windom, Eolus, and Sunlight—three of Colorado's elite Fourteeners.

Twenty-five miles north of Durango, the Skyway finds the first of two destination ski resorts—Purgatory. From November to April, Purgatory boasts some of the deepest powder in the state. Its trail system makes it one of the best family-oriented ski mountains in the Southwest. Snowboarding and telemark skiing are popular alternatives to conventional skiing here. And, to draw visitors back in the summer, Purgatory hosts an annual chamber music festival and it is developing a prodigious system of mountain bike trails.

Left: Durango's Fiesta Days parade, held each July, is but one of many civic festivities that take place each summer along the Skyway. During September and October, all towns along the drive join together to observe Colorfest, a month-long celebration of autumn's colors.

Below: Ned Overend, the three-time national mountain bike champion and twice winner of the World title, finds Durango a great place to ride, race, and live.

Two miles beyond Purgatory, 12,968-foot Engineer Mountain rises directly ahead, while 13,738-foot Grizzly Peak looms in the distance to the left. After crossing Cascade Creek, the Skyway begins its final and most direct assault on Coal Bank Hill, the first of four mountain passes over 10,000 feet. Coal Bank offers the greatest challenge to both racers during the Iron Horse Bicycle Classic on Memorial Day weekend and to automobile cooling systems. From the summit, Pass Creek Trail takes off to the west, accessing a climb up Engineer Mountain.

As the Skyway drops down the other side of Coal Bank, it enters the Lime Creek Burn. Engulfing 26,000 acres in 1879, this large fire stripped many of the surrounding hillsides of trees. Aspen naturally filled in the gap, as did planted evergreens. As an experiment, lodge pole pine, a non-native species, was successfully planted across much of the burn area.

Upon crossing Lime Creek, the road makes a quick climb up Molas Pass. At 10,910 feet, Molas Pass opens up a vast panorama of lofty summits that includes the Continental Divide to the east. Big and Little Molas Lakes, and nearby Andrews Lake, are favored fishing holes here. And the 470-mile Colorado Trail passes through on its way to Denver.

Under the guidance of Gudy Gaskill, the Colorado Trail was built almost entirely by volunteer efforts. Beginning in 1974, the trail was essentially completed by 1988, but the work continues. Access trails are needed and some stretches require upgrading. A system of back country huts is also in the planning stages.

Molas Pass has recently earned the distinction of having the cleanest air in the nation. With the help of a special monitoring camera, the Forest Service has determined that this part of the country contains the fewest particulates, allowing views that can extend up to 170 miles.

From Molas Pass, the Skyway begins a fast descent into Silverton. Since the road skirts precipices several hundred feet high, it is best to pay attention to your driving and save the sightseeing for one of the pullouts along the way. From these overlooks, a marvelous view of Silverton is afforded far below. Nestled along the Animas River between steep mountainsides, the town looks much like a fairy tale town from the Alps.

Right: Snowboarding has become a popular alternative to conventional skiing at Purgatory Resort. This boarder caught some air in Purgatory's "half pipe," an elongated dish of snow where competitors earn points for their acrobatic prowess.

Left: The double jack competition is one of several contests in Silverton's annual Hardrockers Holidays. Double jacking is a method for drilling holes in rock used before the invention of power drills.

The Telluride Fire Hose Team stands ready for competition in downtown Telluride. Such teams were not only important during the 19th century in combatting fires, but were a source of civic pride as well. (Courtesy of Homer E. Reid.)

Situated at 9,300 feet, Silverton has retained much of its original personality. Designated as a national historic landmark, virtually the entire town was built around the turn of the century. Beyond its well-preserved architectural facade, however, Silverton is rare in that it still counts mining as its most important bread winner. Employing some 200 people year-round, the Sunnyside Mine north of town is a major producer of gold.

Of course to thousands of summer visitors, it is Silverton's special ambience that is foremost. The D&SNGR is certainly an integral part of its character, as the train disembarks passengers here each day from May through October. But too, Silverton hosts Hardrockers Holidays—a celebration of mining skills, both past and still practiced. The Kendall Mountain Run has become an important stopover in Colorado's mountain running circuit. And a gathering of brass bands, as well, makes a yearly appearance here.

Following Mineral Creek west, the San Juan Skyway leaves Silverton to begin climbing up 11,008-foot Red Mountain Pass, the literal high point of the trip.

Ouray's Fourth of July celebration includes an unusual competition between the fire companies of Ouray and Ridgway where the idea is to wear out your opponents with a spray of water. Fire posed a constant threat to these mountain towns during the early years, adding historical precedence to the work that volunteer crews do today.

Mountain bicyclists take in the scenery along the Alpine Loop.

the alpine loop: a true back country experience

Whereas the Forest Service has established the scenic byways system, the Bureau of Land Management has been designating its own system of scenic drives, known as back country byways. One of the most alluring of these—the Alpine Loop—is accessible from Silverton.

Sixty-three miles in length, the Alpine Loop circles through an area locals refer to as the San Juan Triangle. From the ghost town of Animas Forks the Loop crosses over 12,600-foot Cinnamon Pass. From there it drops thirty miles to Lake City, a nineteenth-century mining town that today offers a quaint Victorian setting. It was near Lake City in the winter of 1873 that the infamous Alfred Packer made a bit of history by eating his companions. From Lake City, the route climbs over 12,800-foot Engineer Pass to eventually close the circle via Mineral Point. Designated side routes connect the Alpine Loop with Ouray and Silverton. Although some stretches are passable to conventional vehicles, a four-wheel drive is needed to cross the passes. Despite the rough ride, this driving adventure reveals much more of the San Juan Mountains.

This is also the start of the fabled Million Dollar Highway. Along the way, the road passes South Mineral Creek with a spectacular hike into Ice Lake Basin. And, at the base of the pass itself, are the handful of cabins that now mark Chattanooga, once a small mining camp.

Red Mountain Pass marks the dividing line between two watersheds, the San Juan and the Uncompahgre, and two national forests by the same names. Leaving behind the San Juan National Forest, the Skyway winds through the Uncompahgre National Forest until it crosses back over at Lizard Head Pass. (National Forest boundaries often follow those of watersheds.)

In the next twelve miles, the road traces some rather improbable hairpin turns and passes by the now-defunct sites of some once-booming mining camps. Formerly home to thousands, Red Mountain Town, Red Mountain City, Guston, and Ironton had all the amenities: a post office, general stores, and of course, several saloons. Today, the recently closed Idarado mine, along with a flurry of older ruins that dot the hillsides, are all that remain.

After following a rare couple of miles of straight road through Ironton Park, the Skyway enters the Uncompahgre Gorge. Arcing through more hairpin turns, the road drops with deft precision through an incredibly rugged canyon. This stretch of the road was first punched through by Otto Mears, despite the doubts of his contemporaries. Even today, engineers marvel at Mears's handiwork.

Part way down, the road passes through the Riverside Slide snowshed. The Skyway, from Silverton to Ouray, has the dubious distinction of having more potential for avalanches than any other road in North America, and before a snowshed was built, the Riverside Slide claimed many lives. Each winter the state highway department is faced with the monumental task of keeping these roads passable and safe. After heavy snows, the road is closed temporarily so that crews can trigger slides with artillery guns. Plows then move in to clean off the snow.

Preceding pages: The Ouray Hot Springs Pool has offered a popular way to relax since 1926. In December the waters are rendered especially inviting by cold outdoor temperatures and Christmas lights. **Inset:** *A mother and daughter find the Ouray Hot Springs Pool an ideal place to learn about swimming.*

to montrose and beyond

As the Skyway turns west at Ridgway, U.S. Highway 550 continues north, eventually finding the town of Montrose. Montrose lies on the southern edge of one of Colorado's richest agricultural areas where annual harvests of fruits and vegetables are reason enough to pay the area a visit in late summer and early fall.

But too, Montrose is home to the Ute Indian Museum—a storehouse of relics dedicated to Chief Ouray and the Utes—and it is the gateway to one of the most impressive geological treasures in the country, the Black Canyon of the Gunnison. With its most spectacular stretch protected as a national monument, the Black Canyon of the Gunnison stretches fifty-three miles and slices 2,200 feet into dark schist and gneiss rock formations. Measurements from rim to rim are a mere 1,100 feet in places. Although some canyons are deeper and longer, no other can match the Black Canyon for its narrowness and sheer stature. Twelve miles east of Montrose, the Black Canyon of the Gunnison is a natural wonder not to be missed.

The Black Canyon of the Gunnison is a short drive from Montrose.

Dropping 3,200 feet from the pass, the Skyway finally comes to rest in the town of Ouray. Tucked between steep mountainsides, Ouray sprang from strikes made during the 1870s. The fabulous Camp Bird Mine, west of town, produced tens of millions of dollars in gold, making it one of the richest gold strikes in the West. The wife of the mine's original owner later bought the Hope Diamond.

Today, Ouray is a popular base camp for four wheelers and hikers alike. A jeep road tops 13,114-foot Imogene Pass, offering a shortcut of sorts to Telluride. And Yankee Boy Basin, aside from providing access to Mount Sneffels, is also known for its summer spectacle of wildflowers. Within Ouray, a number of beautiful Victorian buildings line the streets. Annual events include a Fourth of July celebration, the Jeepers Jamboree, and a culinary art show. Constituting the town's biggest attraction are the relaxing waters of its hot springs. Piped into an olympic-sized, city-owned pool, Ouray's fabled mineral waters have lured visitors to stop for many years.

Temporarily leaving the mountains beyond Ouray, the Skyway enters lush pasture land before reaching Ridgway. Although its roots were as a railroad town, Ridgway soon became a hub for area cowboys, and it is ranching that typifies the town today. Capitalizing on Ridgway's old West character, Hollywood filmed some memorable westerns here, including *True Grit* and *How The West Was Won.* At Ridgway, the San Juan Skyway leaves U.S. 550 to head west on State Highway 62. Just out of town, the road begins climbing up 8,970-foot Dallas Divide. Once on top, the view south is spectacular. Interrupting the big blue sky are the rugged profiles of 14,150-foot Mount Sneffels and several slightly smaller peaks. One of the most photographed in the West, this vista is the stereotypical calender shot, spring, fall, or winter.

At Placerville, where the route meets the San Miguel River, the drive takes up State Road 145 and travels towards Telluride. Actually a couple of miles off the Skyway, Telluride is tucked away in a deep box canyon. So stunning is its locale that John Naisbitt, author of the best seller *Megatrends* and full-time resident of Telluride, called the town the "most beautiful place on the planet."

In part because of its incredible locale, Telluride has become a mountain community of international repute. Skiing is, of course, a prime attraction here, as the nearby slopes offer a range of downhill challenges. Of these, the "Plunge" and the "Spiral Stairs" are two runs that experts rank among the toughest. But aside from its superb skiing, Telluride has also become known as the "Festival Capital of Colorado." During the off-season, the town hosts an array of theme gatherings to satisfy most any interest. In June comes the Bluegrass Festival. July brings the jazz and ideas festivals. August is time for chamber music and mushroom gathering. And September ushers in an acclaimed film festival, photo workshops, and a hang gliding competition.

For all of Telluride's cosmopolitan flare, it might be easy to forget that this town had its start as a mining camp in the 1800s. But Telluride has retained much of its nineteenth-century personality. Like Silverton, Telluride is a national historic landmark, and a few good historical yarns originated in Telluride. Butch Cassidy robbed his first bank here on June 24, 1889. And the town's name, although borrowed from a gold bearing ore, was often altered to read "To Hell You Ride," a reference to the harrowing train ride into town.

Leaving Telluride behind, the Skyway begins a steady ascent up Lizard Head Pass. Along the way, a few more fourteeners—including Mount Wilson and Wilson Peak—come into view to the southwest. About halfway up, a turn to the left leads to Ophir. Towering nearby are the Ophir Needles, a favorite haunt for rock climbers. To the right, another gravel road drops to the Ames Power Plant. Constructed in 1891 and powered by a flume from Trout Lake above, this power station produced the world's first commercial supply of alternating current. Offering

Left: Downtown Telluride is a montage of Victorian store-fronts. Butch Cassidy robbed his first bank here in 1889.

Below: Wayne Shorter, former saxophone player for the group Weather Report, plays some hot licks at the 1989 Telluride Jazz Festival. This three-day gathering of world renowned musicians, along with several other summertime festivals, has placed Telluride on the map as the festival capital of Colorado.

four corners country

In the desert country that spills south and west from Cortez yawns a vast panorama of striking landmarks and wide open spaces. At the heart of this land is the Four Corners Monument, the only place in the nation where four states meet. For all its singularity, however, the importance of this joining of four sovereignties pales by comparison to the scenic and cultural sights that abound in the region.

In New Mexico rises an enormous volcanic dike known as Shiprock. Anchoring Colorado's Ute Mountain Ute Reservation is Sleeping Ute Mountain—a dormant giant according to Indian legend. Along the Colorado and Utah border are the prehistoric towers of Hovenweep National Monument. Left centuries before by the Anasazi culture, these ruins are reminders that this desert land once supported a much larger population

than it does today. Sprawling across southern Utah is a vast wilderness of slickrock canyons highlighted by five national parks. And in adjacent Arizona lies the bulk of the Navajo Nation, the largest Indian reservation in the country and a prodigious source of Native American crafts. The Four Corners country, topped by a big blue sky, is a pleasurable anomaly of western America.

Far Left: Rising abruptly in northwestern New Mexico, Shiprock has inspired many a legend. According to the Navajo, the landmark represents a great bird that brought their people from the north.

Left: Windsurfing is simply one of many water-sports that have found a home on the waters of McPhee Reservoir near Dolores. This windsurfer is setting a course under the late afternoon sun.

Below: A cattle roundup near Cherry Creek, between Mancos and Durango, recalls the Old West lure of the region as depicted in the books of the late Louis L'Amour, a long-time resident of the area.

This photo of the Ute Chief Sevara and his family, taken in 1899, depicts typical Ute garb at the turn of the century. (Courtesy of the Fort Lewis College Center for Southwest Studies.)

considerable savings to area mines back then, the Ames station still produces electricity today.

Continuing on, the Skyway passes Trout Lake before topping out on 10,222-foot Lizard Head Pass. Although gentle enough that narrow gauge tracks of the Rio Grande Southern line once crossed over it, Lizard Head Pass is surrounded by peaks that are quite rugged. To the east is Pilot's Knob, the Golden Horn, Vermilion Peak, and Sheep Mountain, all over 13,000 feet. Immediately west of the road sits Black Face, a long, gentle ridge. And behind it, out of view from the pass but visible a little ways further, loom the San Miguel Mountains. Encompassed by the Lizard Head Wilderness Area, this sub-range of the San Juans includes a curious protrusion of rock known as Lizard Head. Because the rock is so unstable, this chimney-like formation is ranked as Colorado's hardest climb.

At Lizard Head Pass, the Skyway begins the long, slow drop along the Dolores River. The first miles wind gently through open parkland, but eventually, the scenery takes up forests of spruce and fir and extensive stands of aspen.

After a few miles, the Skyway reaches the mining town of Rico. Established atop a rich find, the town prospered for several years. Today, Rico is a quiet little cluster of buildings, including the old Dolores County Courthouse. Since the county seat moved to Dove Creek some years back, the old building now serves as the town hall and as an architectural embellishment worthy of a visit.

Just south of Rico, on the right are some peculiar beehive structures. These are coke ovens constructed as part of an early smelting process; they are an oddity in the San Juans. On the left, a bit further, the old Scotch Creek Toll Road takes off. Connecting Rico with Rockwood, this route constituted an important link to the outside world until the railroad rendered it obsolete in 1891.

For several more miles the Skyway descends, passing a number of forest access roads, including the one up the West Dolores River, a stream much revered by fly fishermen. About fifty miles from Lizard Head Pass is the town of Dolores. It was near this spot that Escalante named the Dolores River after "Our Lady of Sorrows." Today, Dolores benefits from ranching and logging in the area. And recently, the town has also become known as the gateway to McPhee Reservoir, one of Colorado's largest man-made lakes. Of course, McPhee is a boating and fishing paradise. But too, before the dam was closed, a massive archaeological effort removed the remains of countless Anasazi sites. Many of these artifacts are now on display, along with a set of ruins, at the Anasazi Heritage Center three miles past Dolores on State Road 184.

At the town of Cortez, the Skyway drops to its low elevation of 6,200 feet. Cortez has always been an agricultural community, relying on ranching and the cultivation of pinto beans as a means of support. An energy boom in the 1970s added to its fortune. Of interest to visitors, however, are the many cultural resources nearby. Cortez, in fact, bills itself as the "Archaeological Center of the United States." West of the city is the Crow

These Anasazi ruins are found at the Chimney Rock Archaeological Area.

east to pagosa springs

Upon returning to Durango, you may want to explore more of the San Juan country. If so, a logical direction to head would be east towards Pagosa Springs. Following U.S. Highway 160, you will soon arrive in the small town of Bayfield. North of Bayfield is Vallecito Reservoir, a boating and fishing hot spot. And to the south and southwest is the Southern Ute Indian Reservation, Colorado's other Ute nation. At tribal headquarters in nearby Ignacio, you can pay a visit to the Southern Ute Indian Cultural Center. Or you might catch one of many horse events at Sky Ute Downs.

About halfway to Pagosa Springs rises the appropriately named Chimney Rock. The Anasazi built several dwellings at the base of the rock, and tours of these ruins are available through the San Juan National Forest. At Pagosa Springs itself, you can experience the charm of a quiet mountain community. Named after an Indian word that means "healing waters," Pagosa Springs has so many hot mineral springs that its public buildings are heated geothermically. Beyond town beckon the alluring mountain lands of Wolf Creek Pass and the South San Juans: one more tank of gas and still another driving adventure.

Canyon Archaeological Center where visitors can sign up for a week of excavating ruins with professional archeologists. To the south is the Ute Mountain Ute Reservation, which includes a large tribal park that offers tours of cliff dwellings. And to the east rises the grand escarpment of Mesa Verde National Park.

Mesa Verde, located 10 miles east of Cortez along the Skyway, is indeed the nation's premier archaeological park. Established in 1906, Mesa Verde National Park covers 52,000 acres of pristine mesa and canyon country. Tucked away in alcoves are many cliff dwellings, the best known of which include Balcony House, Spruce Tree House, Long House, and Cliff Palace. In 1978 Mesa Verde became a United Nations World Heritage Cultural Site, making it an important stop for foreign tourists.

Sharing the claim of being the gateway to Mesa Verde is the picturesque town of Mancos, a small ranching community eight miles east of the park turn-off. It was from Mancos that ranchers Richard Wetherill and Charles Mason rode when they discovered Cliff Palace in a December 1888 snow storm. The Wetherill ranch is still in operation near Mancos. On the west end of Mancos, the Skyway passes a mill where aspen logs were once turned into matchsticks. Also in Mancos is the turn-off for State Highway 184. Following a portion of the route Dominguez and Escalante took in 1776, this road doubles back to the Skyway near Dolores. Accessing some beautiful ranch country, this route passes a number of forest roads, several great fishing lakes, and even a couple of llama farms.

From the Mancos Valley, the Skyway climbs Mancos Hill and crosses into the Cherry Creek area. This is where western author Louis L'Amour made his home for several years, and much of this landscape made it into his books. The La Plata Mountains, a sub-range of the San Juans, rise to the north, with some summits topping the 13,000-foot level. At the crossroads of Hesperus, a turn to the north will take you up La Plata Canyon for several miles. Walled in by steep peaks, the drive is a spectacular one highlighted by beautiful mountain scenery and a handful of abandoned and working mines. Although passable to most vehicles for much of the way, the last three miles to Kennebec Pass do require a four-wheel drive. All efforts are well rewarded, though, by the views from the top.

From Hesperus, the Skyway drops back into Durango to close the circle. A mere 236 miles, perhaps, but an entire lifetime of wondrous things to see and experience.

Left: At the base of Wilson Peak, verdant meadows are interspersed with stands of spruce. Such open areas are great places to spot deer and elk on summer evenings.

Below: Early morning finds a dusting of fresh snow on a back road near Mancos. Mancos Valley proffers many such scenes of rural beauty.

Scott S. Warren

A long-time resident of southwestern Colorado, Scott S. Warren has come to know the San Juan Mountains quite well. As a freelance photographer and writer, his work has appeared in such national publications as *Americana, Audubon, National Geographic World, National Parks, Outside,* and *Sierra* magazines. His photos illustrated the book *Enemy Ancestors,* and he photographed and co-wrote with his wife, Beth, the book *Victorian Bonanza.*

Backpacking is one of the more time-honored means of visiting the San Juan back country. Sunrise found this solitary wilderness visitor in Ice Lake Basin.